THE WISDOM OF JESUS

THE WISDOM OF JESUS

Compiled by Philip Law
Introduced by Tom Wright

Heaven and earth will pass away,
but my words will never pass away.

Luke 21:33

William B. Eerdmans Publishing Company
Grand Rapids, Michigan

Copyright © 1996 Lion Publishing

This edition published 1996 in the USA
through special arrangement with
Lion Publishing by
Wm. B. Eerdmans Publishing Co.
255 Jefferson Ave. S.E., Grand Rapids,
Michigan 49503

Printed in Singapore

01 00 99 98 97 96   7 6 5 4 3 2 1

ISBN 0-8028-3832-4

CONTENTS

INTRODUCTION

'No one ever spoke like this man,' said the Temple guards, explaining why they hadn't been able to arrest Jesus. 'They were astonished at his teaching,' wrote one of Jesus' biographers. 'Well said, Teacher,' commented someone who had come to criticize.

What was it that amazed the soldiers, astonished the hearers, and confounded the critics? Read through this book and you'll see. If it's wisdom you're after, this is where to start.

Why is Jesus such an extraordinary teacher? His followers, then and now, regard him as the Son of God. But these teachings are not lofty pronouncements, detached from real life. This is astute wisdom of the highest class.

Hardly surprising, really. It comes out of one of the richest traditions of wisdom in the world. The Jewish Scriptures (which Christians call the Old Testament) are full of poetry, prophecy, and wisdom that cast a clear, healing beam of light on the often murky world of day-to-day living.

Jesus was soaked in these writings, and drew them together in a fresh way.

What's more, Jesus believed that the long story of God and Israel was reaching its climax in his own work. The prophecies would come true: God would teach his people a wisdom that would guide them not simply through this world but on into the new one he was bringing to birth. What you now hold in your hand is a compressed and compelling summary of his message.

Jesus' wisdom, then, isn't just good advice. It's good news. It isn't a set of commands; it's an invitation to open your heart to God's love, to God's call. And with that loving call goes a new strength, a new motivation. Jesus defeated evil. He pioneered a new way of life. This wisdom tells you how you can be part of it.

But there's more. In this wisdom you will find a thumbnail sketch of Jesus himself. His story about a father welcoming a renegade son illustrates and explains his own welcome of outcasts. In the summons to be as wise as a serpent and innocent as a dove we can see a portrait of the speaker.

When he spoke of God's astonishing love, he was also living it out; and, in his death, he acted it out as fully as could be imagined. That's part of what 'Son of God' really means.

Take time, then, over this book. Roll the

phrases around your mouth. Taste their subtle flavour; refresh yourself with the freedom and love they contain.

You might like to learn some of them by heart. You might take a page each day, and think and pray about what it might mean in your life. Above all, you might find yourself coming to recognize the person who stands behind the words. Part of the point of Jesus saying them in the first place was in order to invite people, not just to live by a new wisdom but to share his own love and life.

TOM WRIGHT

Lichfield Cathedral
February 1996

PROLOGUE

In the beginning was the Word,
and the Word was with God,
and the Word was God.
He was in the beginning with God.
All things came into being through him,
and without him not one thing came into being.
In him was life,
and the life was the light of all people.
The light shines in the darkness,
and the darkness has not overcome it.
The Word became flesh and lived among us,
and we have seen his glory,
the glory of the Father's only Son,
full of grace and truth.

John 1:1–5, 14

TRUE
WISDOM

I

Be wise as serpents
and innocent as doves.

Matthew 10:16

THE TWO GREAT COMMANDMENTS

A lawyer asked Jesus a question, saying,
'Master, which is the great commandment in the law?'
Jesus said unto him,
' "Thou shalt love the Lord thy God with all thy heart,
and with all thy soul, and with all thy mind."
This is the first and great commandment.
And the second is like unto it,
"Thou shalt love thy neighbour as thyself." '

Matthew 22:35–39

ABANDON YOUR SELF

What good is it for a man to gain the whole world,
yet forfeit his soul?
Or what can a man give in exchange for his soul?

Mark 8:36–37

In very truth I tell you,
unless a grain of wheat falls
into the ground and dies,
it remains that and nothing more;
but if it dies, it bears a rich harvest.
Whoever loves himself is lost,
but he who hates himself in this world
will be kept safe for eternal life.

John 12:24–25

The Soul Belongs to God

Then he told them a parable:

'There was once a rich man who, having had a good harvest from his land, thought to himself, "What am I to do? I have not enough room to store my crops."

'Then he said, "This is what I will do: I will pull down my barns and build bigger ones, and store all my grain and my goods in them, and I will say to my soul: My soul, you have plenty of good things laid by for many years to come; take things easy, eat, drink, have a good time."

'But God said to him, "Fool! This very night the demand will be made for your soul; and this hoard of yours, whose will it be then?"

'So it is when someone stores up treasure for himself instead of becoming rich in the sight of God.'

Luke 12:16–21

BORN OF THE SPIRIT

Now there was a man named Nicodemus, a member of the Jewish ruling council. He came to Jesus at night and said, 'Rabbi, we know you are a teacher who has come from God.' In reply Jesus declared, 'I tell you the truth, no-one can see the kingdom of God unless he is born again.'

'How can a man be born when he is old?' Nicodemus asked. 'Surely he cannot enter a second time into his mother's womb!'

Jesus answered, 'I tell you the truth, no-one can enter the kingdom of God unless he is born of water and the Spirit. Flesh gives birth to flesh, but the Spirit gives birth to spirit. You should not be surprised at my saying, "You must be born again." The wind blows wherever it pleases. You hear its sound, but you cannot tell where it comes from or where it is going. So it is with everyone born of the Spirit.'

John 3:1–8

6

BECOME LIKE LITTLE CHILDREN

He called a little child and had him stand
among them.

And he said: 'I tell you the truth, unless
you change and become like little children, you
will never enter the kingdom of heaven.
Therefore, whoever humbles himself like this
child is the greatest in the kingdom of heaven.'

Matthew 18:2–4

TRUE HAPPINESS

7

There is more
happiness in giving
than in receiving.

Acts 20:35

DO NOT BE WORRIED

Do not be worried about the food and drink
you need in order to stay alive,
or about clothes for your body.
After all, isn't life worth more than food?
And isn't the body worth more than clothes?
Look at the birds: they do not sow seeds,
gather a harvest and put it in barns;
yet your Father in heaven takes care of them!

Aren't you worth much more than birds?
Can any of you live a bit longer
by worrying about it?
And why worry about clothes?
Look how the wild flowers grow:
they do not work or make clothes for themselves.
But I tell you that not even King Solomon
with all his wealth had clothes as beautiful
as one of these flowers.

So do not start worrying:
'Where will my food come from?
or my drink? or my clothes?'
Instead, be concerned above everything else with the
Kingdom of God and with what he requires of you,
and he will provide you with all these other things.

Do not worry about tomorrow;
it will have enough worries of its own.
There is no need to add to the troubles each day brings.

Matthew 6:25–34

BE HAPPY!

Happy are those who are spiritually poor;
the Kingdom of heaven belongs to them!
Happy are those who mourn;
God will comfort them!
Happy are those who are humble;
they will receive what God has promised!
Happy are those whose greatest desire is
to do what God requires;
God will satisfy them fully!
Happy are those who are merciful to others;
God will be merciful to them!
Happy are the pure in heart;
they will see God!
Happy are those who work for peace;
God will call them his children!
Happy are those who are persecuted
because they do what God requires;
the Kingdom of heaven belongs to them!

Matthew 5:3–10

HEAVENLY TREASURE

The Kingdom of heaven is like this.
A man happens to find a treasure hidden in a field.
He covers it up again, and is so happy that he goes
and sells everything he has,
and then goes back and buys that field.

Matthew 13:44

For where your treasure is,
there will your heart be also.

Matthew 6:21

FIND YOUR TRUE SELF

There was a man who had two sons. The younger of them said to his father, 'Father, give me the share of the property that will belong to me.' So he divided his property between them. A few days later the younger son gathered all he had and travelled to a distant country, and there he squandered his property in dissolute living. When he had spent everything, a severe famine took place throughout that country, and he began to be in need. So he went and hired himself out to one of the citizens of that country, who sent him to his fields to feed the pigs. He would gladly

have filled himself with the pods that the pigs were eating; and no one gave him anything.

But when he came to himself he said, 'How many of my father's hired servants have bread enough and to spare, but here I am dying of hunger! I will get up and go to my father, and I will say to him, "Father, I have sinned against heaven, and before you; I am no longer worthy to be called your son; treat me like one of your hired servants."

So he set off and went to his father. But while he was still far off, his father saw him and was filled with compassion; he ran and put his arms around him and kissed him. Then the son said to him, 'Father, I have sinned against heaven and before you; I am no longer worthy to be called your son.' But the father said to his slaves, 'Quickly, bring out a robe—the best one—and put it on him; put a ring on his finger and sandals on his feet. And get the fatted calf and kill it, and let us eat and celebrate; for this son of mine was dead and is alive again; he was lost and is found!'

Luke 15:11–24

THE JOY OF LOVE

Jesus said to his disciples,
'As the Father has loved me,
so I have loved you;
abide in my love.
If you keep my commandments,
you will abide in my love,
just as I have kept my Father's commandments
and abide in his love.
I have said these things to you
so that my joy may be in you,
and that your joy may be complete.
This is my commandment,
that you love one another as I have loved you.
No one has greater love than this,
to lay down one's life for one's friends.
You are my friends if you do what I command you.
I do not call you servants any longer,
but I have called you my friends,
because I have made known to you
everything that I have heard
from my Father.'

John 15:9–15

TRUE PRAYER

___3___

Whatever you ask for
in prayer,
believe that you have
received it,
and it will be yours.

Mark 11:24

THE LORD'S PRAYER

This is how you should pray:
Our Father in heaven,
may your name be hallowed;
your kingdom come,
your will be done,
on earth as in heaven.
Give us today our daily bread.
Forgive us the wrong we have done,
as we have forgiven those who have wronged us.
And do not put us to the test,
but save us from the evil one.

Matthew 6:9–13

GOD HEARS

Ask, and it will be given to you;
search, and you will find;
knock, and the door will be opened to you.
For everyone who asks receives;
everyone who searches finds;
everyone who knocks will have the door opened.
What father among you,
if his son asked for a fish, would hand him a snake?
Or if he asked for an egg, hand him a scorpion?
If you then, evil as you are,
know how to give your children what is good,
how much more will the heavenly Father
give the Holy Spirit to those who ask him!

Luke 11:9–13

GOD KNOWS

When you pray, do not be like the hypocrites!
They love to stand up and pray in the houses of worship,
so that everyone will see them.
I assure you, they have already been paid in full.
But when you pray, go to your room, close the door,
and pray to your Father, who is unseen.
And your Father, who sees what you do in private,
will reward you.
When you pray, do not use a lot of meaningless words.
Your Father already knows what you need
before you ask him.

Matthew 6:5–8

GOD IS MERCIFUL

Two men went up to the Temple to pray,
one a Pharisee, the other a tax collector.
The Pharisee stood there
and said this prayer to himself,
'I thank you, God, that I am not grasping, unjust,
adulterous like everyone else,
and particularly that I am not like
this tax collector here.'
The tax collector stood some distance away,
not daring even to raise his eyes to heaven;
but he beat his breast and said,
'God, be merciful to me, a sinner.'
This man, I tell you, went home again justified;
the other did not.
For everyone who raises himself up will be humbled,
but anyone who humbles himself will be raised up.

Luke 18:10–14

THE SPIRIT IS WILLING

They came to a place called Gethsemane, and Jesus said to his disciples, 'The sorrow in my heart is so great that it almost crushes me. Stay here and keep watch.'

He went a little farther on, threw himself on the ground, and prayed that, if possible, he might not have to go through that time of suffering.

'Father,' he prayed, 'my Father! All things are possible for you. Take this cup of suffering away from me. Yet not what I want, but what you want.'

Then he returned and found the disciples asleep. And he said to them, 'Keep watch, and pray that you will not fall into temptation. The spirit is willing, but the flesh is weak.'

Mark 14:32–38

TRUE
LOVE

19

Do to others as you
would have them
do to you:
for this is the Law and
the Prophets.

Matthew 7:12

LOVE DOES NOT JUDGE

Do not judge, and you will not be judged.
Do not condemn, and you will not be condemned.
Forgive, and you will be forgiven.
Give, and it will be given to you.
A good measure, pressed down, shaken together
and running over, will be poured into your lap.
For with the measure you use,
it will be measured to you.

Why do you look at the speck of sawdust in your
brother's eye and pay no attention to
the plank in your own eye?
How can you say to your brother, 'Brother, let me
take the speck out of your eye,' when you yourself
fail to see the plank in your own eye?
You hypocrite, first take the plank out of your
eye, and then you will see clearly to remove the
speck from your brother's eye.

Luke 6:37–38, 41–42

LOVE DOES NOT CONDEMN

At daybreak he appeared again in the temple. He had taken his seat and was engaged in teaching, when the scribes and the Pharisees brought in a woman caught committing adultery. Making her stand in the middle, they said to him, 'Teacher, this woman was caught in the very act of adultery. In the law Moses has laid down that such women are to be stoned. What do you say about it?'

Jesus bent down and wrote with his finger on the ground. When they continued to press their question he sat up straight and said, 'Let whichever of you is free from sin throw the first stone.' Then once again he bent down and wrote on the ground. When they heard what he said, one by one they went away, the eldest first; and Jesus was left alone, with the woman still standing there. Jesus again sat up and said to the woman, 'Where are they? Has no one condemned you?' She answered, 'No one sir.' 'Neither do I condemn you,' Jesus said. 'Go; do not sin again.'

John 8:2–11

LOVE DOES NOT LOOK AWAY

On one occasion an expert in the law stood up to test Jesus. 'Teacher,' he asked, 'what must I do to inherit eternal life?'

'What is written in the Law?' he replied.

He answered: ' "Love the Lord your God with all your heart"; and, "Love your neighbour as yourself." '

'You have answered correctly,' Jesus replied. 'Do this and you will live.' But he wanted to justify himself, so he asked Jesus, 'And who is my neighbour?'

In reply Jesus said: 'A man was going down from Jerusalem to Jericho, when he fell into the hands of robbers. They stripped him of his clothes, beat him and went away, leaving him half-dead. A priest happened to be going down the same road, and when he saw the man, he passed by on the other side. So too, a Levite, when he came to the place, passed by on the other side.

But a Samaritan, as he travelled, came where the man was; and when he saw him, he took pity on him. He went to him and bandaged his wounds, pouring on oil and wine. Then he put the man on his own donkey, brought him to an inn and took care of him. The next day he took out two silver coins and gave them to the innkeeper. 'Look after him,' he said, 'and when I return, I will reimburse you for any extra expense you may have.'

'Which of these three do you think was a neighbour to the man who fell into the hands of robbers?'

The expert in the law replied, 'The one who had mercy on him.'

Jesus told him, 'Go and do likewise.'

Luke 10:25–37

LOVE DOES NOT EXPECT A REWARD

Love your enemies; do good to those who hate you;
bless those who curse you;
pray for those who treat you spitefully.
If anyone hits you on the cheek, offer the other also;
if anyone takes your coat,
let him have your shirt as well.
If you love only those who love you,
what credit is that to you?
Even sinners love those who love them.
If you do good only to those who do good to you,
what credit is there in that?
Even sinners do as much.
But you must love your enemies and do good,
and lend without expecting any return;
and you will have a rich reward:
you will be sons of the Most High,
because he himself is kind to
the ungrateful and the wicked.
Be compassionate,
as your Father is compassionate.

Luke 6:27–36

LOVE WILL ALWAYS FORGIVE

When they came to the place that is
called The Skull,
they crucified Jesus with the criminals,
one on his right and one on his left.
Then Jesus said, 'Father, forgive them;
for they do not know what they are doing.'

Luke 23:33–34

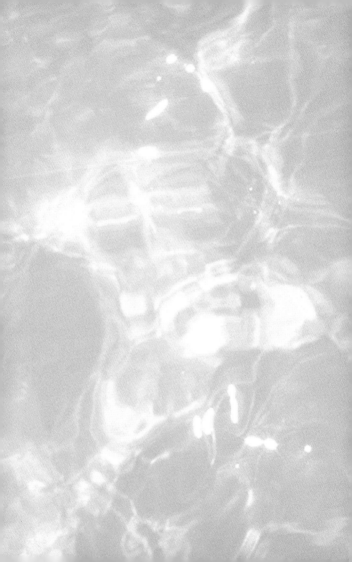

TRUE GOD

25

God is spirit,
and those who
worship him
must worship in spirit
and in truth.

John 4:24

THE INVISIBLE KINGDOM

Some Pharisees asked Jesus when the Kingdom of God would come.

His answer was, 'The Kingdom of God does not come in such a way as to be seen.

No one will say, "Look, here it is!" or, "There it is!"; because the Kingdom of God is within you.'

Luke 17:20–21

THE WAY TO THE FATHER

Jesus said: 'I am the Way; I am Truth and Life.
No one can come to the Father except through me.
If you know me, you will know my Father too.
From this moment you know him and have seen him.'
Philip said, 'Lord, show us the Father
and then we shall be satisfied.'
Jesus said to him, 'Have I been with you all this time,
Philip, and you still do not know me?
'Anyone who has seen me has seen the Father.'

John 14:6–10

THE SPIRIT WITHIN

I will ask the Father, and he will give you another to be your advocate, who will be with you for ever—the Spirit of truth. The world cannot accept him, because the world neither sees nor knows him; but you know him, because he dwells with you and will be in you. I will not leave you bereft; I am coming back to you.

When that day comes you will know that I am in my Father, and you in me and I in you. Anyone who has received my commands and obeys them—he it is who loves me; and he who loves me will be loved by my Father; and I will love him and disclose myself to him.

John 14:16–21

THE PEACE OF GOD

Peace I leave with you; my peace I give you.
I do not give to you as the world gives.
Do not let your hearts be troubled
and do not be afraid.
The world must learn that I love the Father
and that I do exactly what my Father has
commanded me.

John 14:27

I have told you these things, so that in me you
may have peace.
In this world you will have trouble.
But take heart! I have overcome the world.

John 16:33

THE GLORY OF GOD

Then Jesus looked up to heaven and said:
'Father, the hour has come.
Glorify your Son,
that the Son may glorify you.
For you have made him sovereign over all mankind,
to give eternal life to all whom you have given him.
This is eternal life: to know you the only true God,
and Jesus Christ whom you have sent.
I have glorified you on earth by finishing the work
which you gave me to do;
and now, Father, glorify me in your own presence
with the glory which I had with you
before the world began.'

John 17:1–5

EPILOGUE

God so loved the world that he gave his only Son,
that everyone who has faith in him
may not perish but have eternal life.
This is the judgement:
the light has come into the world,
but people preferred darkness to light
because their deeds were evil.
Those who live by the truth come to the light
so that it may be clearly seen that
God is in all they do.

John 3:16, 19, 21

Text Acknowledgments

Extracts from the Authorised Version of the Bible (The King James Bible), the rights of which are vested in the Crown, are reproduced by permission of the Crown's Patentee, Cambridge University Press: pages 14, 34.

Scriptures quoted from the *Good News Bible* published by The Bible Societies/HarperCollins Publishers Ltd UK © American Bible Society, 1966, 1971, 1976, 1992: pages 19, 20-21, 23, 30, 32, 42.

Scripture quotations taken from the HOLY BIBLE, NEW INTERNATIONAL VERSION. Copyright © 1973, 1978, 1984 by International Bible Society. Used by permission of Hodder & Stoughton Ltd. All rights reserved. 'NIV' is a registered trademark of International Bible Society. UK trademark number 1448790: pages 15, 17, 18, 36-37, 45 (twice)

New Jerusalem Bible © 1985 by Darton, Longman and Todd Ltd and Doubleday and Company, Inc.: pages 16, 29, 31, 38, 43.

Scripture text from the New Revised Standard Version of the Bible, copyright © 11989 by the Division of Christian Education of the National Council of the Churches of Christ in the USA: pages 11, 13, 24-25, 26, 27, 33, 39.

Revised English Bible © 1989 by permission of Oxford and Cambridge University Presses: pages 3, 15, 23, 28, 35, 41, 44, 46, 47.

Scripture text from the Revised Standard Version of the Bible, copyright © 1946, 1952, 1971 by the Division of Christian Education of the National Council of the Churches of Christ in the USA.

Picture Acknowledgments

1, 7, 8: FIT58524 T3216 Ms 194 Leaf from an Italian Choral Book: the Resurrection; scenes from the Life of Christ, 14th century, Vellum, Fitzwilliam Museum, University of Cambridge/Bridgeman Art Library, London; 2/3 Chantilly, Mus. Condé,Giraudon; 4: by permission of the President and Fellows of Corpus Christi College; 13, 19, 27, 33, 41 and cover: BON18997 Christ and four saints, altar panel, designed by Burne-Jones, by Thomas Matthews Rooke (1842–1942) Bonhams, London/Bridgeman Art Library, London; 14: CH 21085 Christ washing the disciples' feet, Arezzo, c.1390 by Italian School,(14th century) Christie's, London/Bridgeman Art Library, London; 17: Ms 47682 f.20v by permission of the British Library/Readers Digest; 20: Staatliche Graphische, Munich; 23: by permission of the President and Fellows of Corpus Christi College; 24: Sonia Halliday; 30: by permission of the President and Fellows of Corpus Christi College; 36/37: Foto Scala, Firenze; 39: BL 30926 Add 16997 f.153v Crucifixion by the Boucicaut Master, French, The Chevalier Hours (early 15th century) British · Library, London/Bridgeman Art Library, London; 41: Bridgeman; 43: Chantilly, Mus. Condé, Lauros/Giraudon; 47: The Bodleian Library, Oxford (MS Douce 293, fol. 15v).

Artwork

All artwork by Amanda Barlow